W9-AFE-189

DAVID WRIGHT

SPORTS STARS who give back

GIFTED AND GIVING BASEBALL STAR

by Marty Gitlin

Enslow Publishers, Inc.
40 Industrial Road
Box 398
Berkeley Heights, NJ 07922
USA
http://www.enslow.com

Library of Congress Cataloging-in-Publication Data
Gitlin, Marty.
David Wright : gifted and giving baseball star / Marty Gitlin.
p. cm. – (Sports stars who give back)
Includes bibliographical references and index.
Summary: "A biography of American baseball player David Wright, focusing on his philanthropic activities off the field"–Provided by publisher.
ISBN 978-0-7660-3588-1
1. Wright, David, 1982–Juvenile literature. 2. Infielders (Baseball)–United States–Biography–Juvenile literature. 3. Philanthropists–United States–Biography–Juvenile literature. I. Title.
GV865.W74G57 2010
796.357092–dc22
[B]

2009026184

Printed in the United States of America

102009 Lake Book Manufacturing, Inc., Melrose Park, IL

10 9 8 7 6 5 4 3 2 1

To Our Readers: We have done our best to make sure all Internet addresses in this book were active and appropriate when we went to press. However, the author and the publisher have no control over and assume no liability for the material available on those Internet sites or on other Web sites they may link to. Any comments or suggestions can be sent by e-mail to comments@enslow.com or to the address on the back cover.

♲ Enslow Publishers, Inc. is committed to printing our books on recycled paper. The paper in every book contains between 10% to 30% post-consumer waste (PCW). The cover board on the outside of each book contains 100% PCW. Our goal is to do our part to help young people and the environment too!

Photo credits: David Zalubowski/AP Images, 1, 77; John Bazemore/AP Images, 6; Frank Franklin II/AP Images, 12, 45, 48, 71; Paul Benoit/AP Images, 19; Winslow Townson/AP Images, 22; Bill Kostroun/AP Images, 25; Nati Harnik/AP Images, 28; Tony Gutierrez/AP Images, 39; Al Behrman/AP Images, 42; Kathy Willens/AP Images, 46, 84, 93, 96, 105; Julie Jacobson/AP Images, 58; Nick Wass/AP Images, 61; Bob Jordan/AP Images, 68; Charles Krupa/AP Images, 80; Steve Mitchell/AP Images, 101; Gregory Smith/AP Images, 107

Cover Photo: David Zalubowski/AP Images

CONTENTS

1

DETOUR ON ROAD TO STARDOM

David Wright had his future all mapped out.

He set his own course by slugging baseballs all over the high school fields of northern Virginia. College scouts from around the country buzzed around him, trying to convince the young shortstop to take his tremendous talents to their school.

They were not only impressed with how the kid wearing a Hickory High School uniform handled himself gripping a bat and wearing a glove. Scouts also loved his maturity. They could not believe someone so young could be so focused and respectful.

Hickory baseball coach Steve Gedro could hardly believe it himself.

TAKING NO CHANCES

Wright had a couple unusual habits and superstitions that he considered helpful when he played for Hickory.

He often ate turkey subs from the local Subway restaurant before games. He also wore one teal sock underneath a black sock during games.

"I remember when I would come out to the field to get it ready for batting practice," Gedro recalled. "Scouts would come up to me and tell me about their experiences with David. They would tell me that he always returned their phone calls and that he was a 'yes sir' and 'no sir' kind of kid. David showed the right kind of attitude in the classroom and on the baseball field."[1]

PLANNING THE NEXT STEP

By the late fall of 2000, Wright had already made an important decision. He had decided to accept a scholarship offer from Georgia Tech. He would play baseball and major in engineering.

How could he go wrong? Major League Baseball star Nomar Garciaparra had played with the Yellow Jackets. At that time, so did Mark Teixeira, the reigning College Baseball Player of the Year who would eventually become one of the greatest sluggers in the

Wright was the heir apparent to Mark Teixeira (above) at Georgia Tech.

sport. And, just like Wright, both played shortstop and third base. David Wright had forged his path to greatness and was prepared to ascend to the next level. He had achieved a brilliant .507 batting average with 31 runs batted in as a mere junior, after which he was selected to the Virginia All-State High School Baseball Team for the second consecutive season.

The national media had even taken notice. *Baseball America* ranked him thirty-ninth in the country among all players heading into their senior years, calling him "a hitting machine."[2] And *USA Today* had selected him to its All-America team.

Wright was excited. Among his fondest moments was watching Georgia Tech and other Atlantic Coast Conference (ACC) baseball teams perform on TV. He had visited Auburn and planned to take trips to Florida State and North Carolina. He cancelled both after his experience at Georgia Tech. One stop at Georgia Tech was all he needed.

"I don't think I could pick one word that describes how I feel," he said after signing a letter-of-intent to play with the Yellow Jackets. "I'm ecstatic."

"I went there and fell in love with it," he added. "I could not see myself anywhere else."[3]

Veteran Georgia Tech coach Danny Hall could not see Wright anywhere else, either. He considered Wright to be the plum of his 2001 recruiting class. He already planned on moving Wright from shortstop to third base, where he would replace Teixeira, who was ready to begin his professional career.

"We wanted to get a third baseman in this year's recruiting class," Hall explained. "I've had some people tell me that we are losing the best third baseman [Teixeira] in college baseball, but we've just signed the best third baseman in high school baseball in David Wright."[4]

"We've just signed the best third baseman in high school baseball in David Wright."

—Danny Hall

OTHER OPTIONS

Hall, however, was braced for a disappointment. He knew that Wright was also eligible for the Major League Baseball draft, which was set for June 2001. Like their college counterparts, professional scouts had also shown a great interest in Wright. And unlike their college counterparts, they represented teams that could offer money and a head start on a professional career.

Wright had little inkling until his senior season just how interested major league teams were. He anticipated being chosen somewhere in the middle of the draft, whereupon he would turn down any professional offer and hone his skills at Georgia Tech.

TEAM SUCCESS, TOO

Wright was not the only player on the Hickory Hawks to perform well during his high school career.

In fact, the team advanced all the way to the state semifinals in 2000, Wright's junior season.

His thinking was soon to change. Wright maximized his draft potential with a sensational performance his senior season. He had played exceptionally well as a freshman, sophomore, and junior, but he was magnificent in his final high school year. He batted .538 in 2001—exactly 100 points higher than his high school career average.

TALENTED COMPANY

Wright is in fine company as a Gatorade Virginia High School Player of the Year, an award presented to athletes in several sports.

Among those who have earned the award over the years are past and current professional standouts in baseball (Justin Upton, Michael Cuddyer, Seth Greisinger), football (Thomas Jones, Terry Kirby) and basketball (Josh Smith, J. J. Redick, Grant Hill, Alonzo Mourning, J. R. Reid).

Cuddyer played at Great Bridge just before Wright arrived at Hickory. Wright admitted in high school that he admired the talented Cuddyer for his attitude. Cuddyer went on to star with the Minnesota Twins.

Though more of a line-drive hitter than a power hitter in high school, Wright also slammed 6 home runs as a senior and was named Gatorade Virginia High School Player of the Year and Virginia All-State Player of the Year. For the third consecutive season, he was selected to the All-State team.

Gedro recalled one game in which Wright was a one-man wrecking crew.

"[In 2008 with the Mets] he hit a walk-off home run and a reporter asked him if it was the first time in his career he had hit a home run to win a game," Gedro recalled. "He said yes, but I recall a game against Great Bridge his senior year. He hit a two-run homer in the fourth inning to tie the game at 2–2.

"Then in the eighth inning we had a runner on base and they decided to pitch to David again [instead of walking him intentionally]. He hit a ball over the scoreboard for another home run and we won the game, 4–2. It was the last time we beat Great Bridge until [2008]."[5]

Suddenly, Wright was a hotter prospect than he figured he would be as the draft approached. He talked over the situation with his family and decided he would sign a professional contract if selected in the first or second round.

Wright awaited the Major League Baseball draft anxiously. But he could only dream that he had been selected by the New York Mets, the team for which he had rooted his entire life. He had spent many an evening with his father Rhon watching the Mets play on TV.

The odds were stacked against it. The Mets had expressed an interest in him. But after all, there were thirty major-league teams. What were the chances he would be picked up his beloved Mets?

Quite good, as it turned out.

GETTING DRAFTED

Much to his shock and delight, Wright was indeed chosen by the Mets with the thirty-eighth pick of the 2001 draft. Their contract offer was simply too tempting to pass up. Wright informed Georgia Tech that he would forego the scholarship and begin his professional career immediately.

Gedro was not surprised. He believed that though a college education is always important, Wright's motivation and maturity made signing a contract with the Mets the right decision. He felt that though his dream team selected Wright, having been chosen that high in the draft would have prompted him to turn professional no matter which team had taken him.

"The main thing is that the money offer was so good," Gedro said. "With David being such an intelligent young man, he did not have to go to Georgia Tech and get a degree to succeed in life. You go to college to make a career for yourself and if David could go for it right out of high school, why not? Regardless, I knew he would be wise with his money because he was just that kind of kid.

FIRST CONTRACT

Professional baseball contracts often take a bit of time to be negotiated. The one Wright signed with the Mets was no different. It took a month for the team and Wright's agent to hammer out a deal.

The contract gave Wright a bonus of $960,000.

A TRAINED EYE

The Mets scout who discovered Wright and convinced him to sign a professional contract was Randy Milligan.

Milligan knew plenty about baseball. In fact, he was a former major-league first baseman and outfielder. Milligan played for five different teams during his major-league career from 1987 to 1994, including a brief stint with the Mets. He spent his most productive seasons, however, with the Baltimore Orioles.

"Maybe he was a little surprised that he was picked so high in the draft, but David was so goal-oriented and driven when it came to baseball, I think he knew that he would go pretty high. I had him as a student in physical education way back when he was in eighth grade and even back then, he was definitely goal-oriented and planned well for everything."[6]

Wright was on his way to stardom. But the seeds of his success were planted by his parents, Rhon and Elisa, in their Norfolk home and on the baseball diamonds throughout the area. It was on those ball fields where Wright developed into a tremendous player and in his home where he blossomed into a generous, thoughtful young man.

The Mets drafted Wright with the thirty-eighth pick in the 2001 MLB Draft.

newera
SHEA STADIUM
5

2

DAVID, THE YOUNG GOLIATH

It was five days before Christmas in 1982. And the wait was over. Rhon and Elisa Wright were about to have their first child.

The Virginia couple believed they were ready to assume the great responsibility. Rhon had secured a steady job as an officer in the Norfolk Police Department. He performed so well in his duties that he eventually ascended to the rank of captain. They owned a comfortable home in the Norfolk suburb of Chesapeake.

On December 20, Rhon and Elisa needed to wait no longer to expand their family. It was on that day just before the official beginning of winter that David Allen Wright was born.

Though David was merely an infant, Rhon had already vowed to raise the child with discipline. As a member of the police force, the young father had been witness to tragic stories about misguided youth ruining their lives by breaking the law. He wanted to keep his son on a straight and productive path.

Rhon would enjoy the opportunity to make that same determination three more times. In the years that followed, three more sons were added to the family. Stephen, Matthew, and Daniel became David's younger brothers.

RAISING HIM THE WRIGHT WAY

David was protective of his siblings. They gave him a sense of responsibility he would carry into his adulthood. They would not be a burden to him. Rather, he would look at it as his duty to help those unable to help themselves. His desire to aid the helpless and those less fortunate would become a part of him.

Not that David felt sorry for his brothers. Far from it—the four competed furiously in just about every endeavor. They played ping-pong and video games at home and often took their athletic rivalries to the nearby bowling alley. Those were healthy activities that their parents supported.

But Rhon and Elisa also gave their four sons a sense of priorities. They could partake in sports and games in the evening only when their homework had been completed. And they were also responsible for particular jobs around the house. It was in his home that David gained the work ethic that became downright legendary during his professional baseball career.

"I was pretty strict but it was nothing unrealistic," Rhon said. "They had certain chores, [there were] very high expectations on school and education. Studying came first."[1]

Wright remembers that clearly. But he also recalls a sense of fairness from his parents, who demanded only that their children performed in the classroom to the best of their abilities. And if that did not result in a perfect mark, they were still satisfied.

"It was not a certain grade [my parents expected me to get]," Wright said. "They pushed me if they thought I could do better. So if the best I could do in a class was a C, and it was a hard class and they saw me working, they'd be fine with that. But if they thought I could do better, that's when they'd get mad."[2]

They did not get mad very often at David's academic performance. The oldest Wright brother maintained excellent grades. He felt comfortable enough to take college courses at Hickory High School, which enabled him to sport a grade-point average of higher than 4.0.

And his parents certainly did not need to worry that he would get into trouble. His only run-in with school authorities occurred when he joined in a food

THE SCIENCE GUY

Wright performed well in all his classes, as his perfect grade point average in high school attested.

But his favorite subject was science. He was particularly interested in anatomy, which is the study of the human body. He also enjoyed physiology, which is the study of other life forms.

fight early in his high school career by throwing a hamburger!

Elisa remembers that incident quite well, possibly because such unruly behavior was so rare from her eldest son.

"Once, in the high school cafeteria, another kid hit David with a french fry," Elisa remembered. "David returned fire with a [hamburger] and struck the kid right upside the head."

"David got an in-school suspension," Rhon added. "I read him the riot act. And after David left the kitchen, [Elisa and I] laughed about it."[3]

A BASEBALL BACKGROUND

Then there was baseball, which was no laughing matter to David. He felt a passion for the sport from the time he was old enough to swing a miniature bat. He would beg his grandfather to play Wiffle ball with

PREPARING FOR THE MAJORS

Wright could have registered even better statistics during high school, but refused to use an aluminum bat, which are legal at that level.

Why? Because professionals are required to use wooden bats and Wright wanted to prepare to play Major League Baseball.

On one occasion while playing for the elite traveling team, his teammates were begging him to use an aluminum bat just once. Wright consented, grabbed one, and hit a home run with it. And he never used one again.

him in the backyard or lure Rhon out for a game of catch.

David soaked in the sport whenever given the opportunity. He vaguely recalled watching the 1986 World Series pitting the Boston Red Sox against his father's favorite team, the New York Mets. He was just three years old, but he recalled the thrill Rhon got from seeing the Mets play in and eventually win the championship of baseball.

One reason Rhon adopted the Mets as his team of choice was that their Class Triple-A minor league affiliate played in nearby Tidewater, Virginia. He even patrolled the ballpark during games in his capacity as a police officer. Despite the fact that he was barely

The Mets beat the Red Sox in the 1986 World Series.

out of the toddler stage, David understood his father's rooting interests and rooted for the Mets right along with him. "I don't recall any plays or games, but I do recall my dad's cheering and excitement during that World Series," David said. "If he had his way, he'd still be wearing the same Mets cap and ripped-up team jacket."[4]

CAL RIPKEN, JR.

Though Wright's favorite major league team growing up was the New York Mets, his favorite athlete at that time was Baltimore Orioles shortstop and third baseman Cal Ripken, Jr.

Ripken was one of the most accomplished players in baseball history and definitely the most durable. He started 2,632 consecutive games over sixteen seasons, which is a major-league record.

David also accompanied his father to Tidewater Tides games, which provided a life lesson. He would search for player autographs, but discovered that it was quite difficult to convince the top players to sign his program. Some would refuse or shoo him away.

He understood even at that early age how easy it would have been to simply sign an autograph and how much it meant to children. David would tuck that painful memory away in his mind and spend a great deal of time patiently and cheerfully signing autographs for kids even after he became a star.

Those close to the family remember well watching the six-year-old boy swinging his bat for hours at a ball resting on a tee. He would make only occasional contact, but his love for taking hacks at baseballs was already quite pronounced.

Soon he was making tremendous contact with baseballs far more difficult to hit—those thrown toward home plate by a pitcher. David played for a Little League team called the Green Run Padres. He was skilled enough at age nine to be playing in a league for older kids.

And even though Rhon coached the team, David did not always get his own way. In fact, he wanted badly to play shortstop, but his father stuck him in right field, a position David detested.

Rhon informed him in no uncertain terms that he would have to earn the right to play shortstop, a position that brings with it great responsibility. David would have to show he could make the tough plays required of shortstops.

A ONE-SPORT MAN

Many kids play several sports during their youth, but Wright was not among them.

Wright dabbled in basketball, and among his most beloved athletes was legendary Chicago Bulls star Michael Jordan. But baseball was the only sport he played extensively.

He was also not particularly athletic during his elementary school years.

Wright, a third baseman for the Mets, originally wanted to be a shortstop.

He certainly proved he could eventually. As David ascended through the Little League ranks, he began to separate himself from his peers talent-wise. One coach who noticed was Allan Erbe, who doubled as a scout for the Chicago Cubs. Erbe claims he told fellow scouts in 1994 that David Wright would eventually play Major League Baseball.

FUTURE STARS

The summer baseball team for which Wright played boasted two other players who would become top major-league hitters.

Wright's teammates included future Washington Nationals third baseman Ryan Zimmerman and eventual Tampa Bay Rays outfielder B. J. Upton. Upton was a key player in Tampa Bay's surprising run to the American League championship in 2008.

Wright was only eleven years old at the time.

"No doubt in my mind," Erbe said. "It was a combination of my experience and intuition. But aside from that, he was head and shoulders above every other kid."[5]

The same, perhaps, could have been said about Wright off the field. After all, Rhon and Elisa had made it clear from the time their first son was old enough to understand that what kind of person he became was far more important than the quality of athlete he developed into.

"They did not set out to raise a good baseball player," Wright said. "They wanted to raise a good person."[6]

Those close to Wright believe that mission was accomplished.

"He was head and shoulders above every other kid."

—Allan Erbe

3

GEARING TOWARD GREATNESS

It was late spring in 2003, and Port St. Lucie Mets manager Ken Oberkfell was perplexed. He could not figure out why prized prospect David Wright hit so much better on the road than at home.

It was not a problem that had just cropped up. Wright's batting average in road games was a mind-boggling 100 points higher. There had to be a reason.

There was. Wright was so driven to succeed that he was working too hard. After a bit of research, Oberkfell discovered that Wright was showing up so early to home games and taking so much extra

Wright blasts a home run at the 2006 All-Star Game.

batting practice that he was exhausted by game time. He arrived at away games at the same time as his teammates, which prevented him from taking hundreds of extra swings of the bat and losing energy.

MAN ON A MISSION

From the moment he was drafted by the New York Mets in 2001, Wright was a man on a mission.

"Playing baseball for a living is a dream come true," he said as he began his first full season in professional baseball in April 2002. "This is what I've been working my whole life for, and now I have the chance to show [the Mets] what I can do. I can't wait."[1]

By that time, they had already seen a glimpse of what Wright could do. After signing a contract for nearly $1 million, he joined the Mets' rookie league team in Kingsport, Tennessee. He recorded an impressive .300 batting average with 4 home runs and 17 runs batted in.

That strong performance prompted the Mets to promote Wright past Lower Class A Brooklyn to Class A Columbia. It also justified their faith in him when they selected him in the 2001 draft.

"We believed we did our homework on David and were delighted to have the chance to draft him where we did," said the Mets' Gary LaRocque, assistant general manager and director of amateur scouting. "We had seen him a lot and knew he was a quality young man who will challenge himself to get where he wants to be.

"He comes from a great family situation and has shown he can handle the exposure that comes from being such a highly regarded prospect, which is sometimes unusual for a high school player."[2]

Now the importance of everything Wright did on and off the field would be magnified. After all, he was playing for his own livelihood. Now every at-bat and every play in the field would be evaluated by the fans, managers, and Mets organization. And any mistake he made in his personal life could hurt his opportunity to thrive in the game he loved.

Wright did not want to be a "free swinger." He was not an all-or-nothing hitter who either hit a home run or struck out. He did not believe that approach to hitting was most beneficial to the team. But he also refused to tone down his competitive nature and intensity. Those attributes were what brought him to the edge of greatness in the first

HOLDING HIS POSITION

Most players in both the minor leagues and major leagues will move to a different position on occasion.

Wright was not among them.

He played 389 games during his minor league career and never moved from third base. That streak would continue through his first five years with the Mets.

Discipline on and off the field helps Wright improve.

place. Wright spoke about his mindset both at the plate and in his career as he prepared for his first full season in organized baseball in April 2002.

"I'm disciplined," he said. "That's the single thing I strive most to be at the plate. When I go up there, I look at it as me versus the pitcher. One of us has to win and one of us has to lose. I don't like to lose, so I'm focused 100 percent on what I have to do to win the at-bat.

"I know it will be a big challenge. Teams don't draft the guys that I hit home runs off of [in high school]. They draft [pitchers] that got me out. Every day the pitchers I'll face are going to be top-quality guys, and you have to be prepared physically and mentally.

"A lot of people have cautioned me to tone it back a little bit because it's a long season. I'm an intense player. I give it everything I have and leave it on the field. I know that with 140 games it's more like a marathon than a sprint, but I'm looking forward to every minute of it."[3]

A PREVIEW OF WHAT'S TO COME

The opposing pitchers did not enjoy it as much. In 2002, Wright displayed the all-around talent that would be his trademark for years to come. He not only batted a solid .266 with 11 home runs, but he was among the South Atlantic League leaders with 93 runs batted in, 85 runs scored, 30 doubles, and 21

FILLING THE TROPHY CASE

Wright has earned many honors during both his amateur and professional baseball career.

One of them was the Sterling Award, which he was given for being the best player on the St. Lucie Mets in 2003. Among Wright's achievements that season was leading the Florida State League with 39 doubles.

THANKS, BUT NO THANKS!

Wright received quite an honor while at Binghamton when he was selected to play in the Double-A All-Star Game.

He had to turn down the invitation, however.

Why? Because by the time the game rolled around, Wright had already been promoted to Triple-A!

stolen bases. And he was named Most Valuable Player of his team.

That combination of power and speed would become a staple of Wright's game. The following season at Upper Class A Port St. Lucie, he batted .270 with 15 home runs and 19 stolen bases.

For many players, Class A is as far from the major leagues as Florida is from New York. But it had become apparent by that time that Wright was destined to make his mark with the Mets. And his performance in 2004 confirmed it.

Wright began that season at Class AA Binghamton, which is also in the state of New York. And though the pitching is far superior at that level than it is in Class A, Wright actually hit with greater success.

In fact, the twenty-one-year-old Wright raised his batting average nearly 100 points to .363. In just 223 at-bats, he smashed 10 home runs with 40 runs batted in and 20 stolen bases. It was a remarkable performance considering he participated in about half the number of games as he did the year before.

Though some of the credit belongs to Oberkfell and hitting coach Howard Johnson, sportswriter Scott Lauber believes it is mostly a testament to Wright's talent.

"His age in relation to his success was incredible," said Lauber, who covered the team for the *Binghamton Press & Sun-Bulletin* in 2004. "Not too many kids that age at the Double-A level dominate like that.

"Oberkfell and Johnson, who were also with him at Port St. Lucie, said in May or early June, 'We've been with him long enough to know that he doesn't

TOP-NOTCH TEACHERS

Both Binghamton manager Ken Oberkfell and hitting coach Howard Johnson had been accomplished major-league hitters.

In fact, Johnson spent a significant part of his career with the Mets.

Oberkfell played mostly for St. Louis and Atlanta. He batted a strong .278 during his sixteen-year major-league career.

Johnson spent most of his fourteen-year career with the Mets and was among the top power hitters in the sport. He averaged more than 30 home runs a year from 1987 to 1991.

need to go to Triple-A.' They felt all along that Wright could go straight to the Mets. And the amount of time that he actually spent at Triple-A showed that he did not need to take that step."[4]

But Lauber was even more impressed with Wright as a person.

"I met David in spring training in 2004 and he and I really hit it off," Lauber recalled. "I could see right away that he was very grounded and down-to-earth. Everyone knew that he was going to be playing for the Mets, but you would have never known it by the way he acted and the way he carried himself."[5]

One incident that particularly impressed Lauber occurred on Memorial Day weekend in 2004. Wright and his teammates wore special jerseys in one game that were to be auctioned off to charity. The Wright

MAKING HIS MARK

Every minor league team Wright played for benefited from his talents.

The 2002 Columbia team finished with a 75–64 record and placed second in the South Atlantic League Southern Division. The 2003 St. Lucie Mets won the East Division of the Florida State League with a 77–62 mark. And the 2004 Binghamton Mets also won more games than they lost during Wright's two months with the team.

jersey was considered the most valuable of all, so it was saved for last at the auction.

Wright was one of only a few players to stay for the entire event. And when the bidding for his jersey reached a certain level, he stood up and informed the bidders that if anyone paid a particular price for his jersey, he would take that person out to lunch. The result was that the Wright jersey brought in more money for the charity than any other.

MOVING UP

Two weeks later, Wright was headed for his hometown to play for the Triple-A Norfolk Tides. Though many believed he was ready for the major leagues, the Mets figured playing at a higher level in front of his family and friends would be a stern test.

It would give him the experience of playing under pressure, and there is no greater pressure for a baseball player than playing in New York, the biggest city in America and one in which the media scrutiny can overwhelm young players.

Wright was not yet in "The Show," which is what players call the major leagues. He needed to jump over one more hurdle to get there.

And he would clear it with room to spare.

4

OLD HOME AND NEW HOME

David Wright finished a doubleheader on June 12, 2004, in Bowie, Maryland. Shortly thereafter, he was given some exciting news: He'd been promoted from Double-A Binghamton to the Triple-A Norfolk Tides.

Wright raced to the parking lot after the game with his uniform still on and told family and friends the news. Not only was he one step closer to playing for his beloved New York Mets, but he was also returning to his hometown. He could play in front of the people he loved every time his team played at home.

Wright had earned the trip. He ranked among the Eastern League leaders in just about every offensive category. But he was not the only one thrilled at the news. Tides manager and former New York Mets catcher John Stearns could not wait to place Wright's name into his lineup card.

"I'm very excited about this," Stearns said. "But the main thing is it's the right thing to do for the kid. He had overmatched Double-A [pitching]. He might come here and do well right away and head for the big leagues. From what I hear, he's getting better by leaps and bounds."[1]

Wright would be doing plenty of leaping and bounding in Norfolk. But playing for the Tides meant far more to him than just an opportunity to perform against a higher level of competition. Wright actually attended the first game ever played at the Tides home field of Harbor Park in 1993, when he was ten years old.

NO DISTRACTIONS

Wright understood that although he enjoyed the company of family and friends, returning home to play baseball could result in problems. He did not want those relationships to take his time or concentration away from his goal, which was to be wearing a New York Mets uniform as soon as possible.

Nothing, however, was going to slow down the immensely talented and motivated twenty-one-year-old from landing in New York. In his first game with the Tides, he slammed a double and two singles and

LIVING AT HOME

Wright actually spent most of his time living with his parents when he played with the Norfolk Tides.

He recalled returning home after a game and receiving some good-natured ribbing from his siblings.

"The biggest pressure I had was playing in front of my three younger brothers," Wright said. "We'd been sitting around the kitchen table after the game playing [cards] and they would razz me."

handled seven plays at third base flawlessly. Not bad considering he was a bundle of nerves during batting practice before the game.

"I felt like I was trying to swing the bat 100 miles an hour," said Wright about his first time taking batting practice at Norfolk. "It was one of the worst batting practices I've had this year.

"That [double] was like a 1,000-pound weight being lifted from my shoulders. I've never been this nervous and excited about one game. My goal was to just get a hit. I've had a couple 3-for-4 nights this season, but this tops them all."[2]

Fans streamed to Harbor Park to watch Wright. The crowd numbered nearly 7,000, more than 2,000 of whom bought tickets after they learned that Wright had been promoted from Binghamton. And he not only rewarded them by his performance on the field, but he also stayed after the game to sign autographs for about 150 fans.

Those who believed Wright did not need seasoning at Triple-A and could have ascended from Double-A directly to New York were justified by his performance in Norfolk. Wright not only batted a healthy .298, but he developed into an even better power hitter with the Tides. He slugged 8 home runs in just thirty-one games.

PROMOTION COMMOTION

Soon speculation ran rampant that Wright was indeed about to be promoted to New York. Mets general manager Jim Duquette wanted to make

A ONE-ACT SHOW

How anxious were the fans of Tidewater to see their hometown hero?

When the lineups were announced before the game in which Wright was to make his debut with the Tides, the crowd fell silent as they waited to hear his name. And when they did, they let out a loud cheer.

The fans had virtually nothing else to cheer about that night. Wright banged out three hits, but the Tides lost to Toledo, 13–6.

NOT ALL SMILES IN NEW YORK

One player who expressed disappointment over Wright's promotion was Mets third baseman Ty Wigginton.

After all, Wright was about to displace Wigginton at that position.

Wigginton was moved to first base before being traded a few weeks later to the Pittsburgh Pirates. He later became a valuable player for both Tampa Bay and Houston.

certain his young phenomenon was ready for the jump, because manager Art Howe was not about to sit Wright on the bench for a while to learn the big league game. He was planning on planting Wright at third base and leaving him there for a long time.

The Mets, after all, had been looking for a long-term solution at third base for two generations. The franchise had been in existence since 1962, yet they had never had long-term stability at that position. They did not want to ruin the best third base prospect in the history of the franchise by promoting him before he was prepared to thrive in the major leagues.

By mid-July, they had seen enough to know that Wright was indeed ready. But although Wright had great confidence in his talent, he was not one to toot

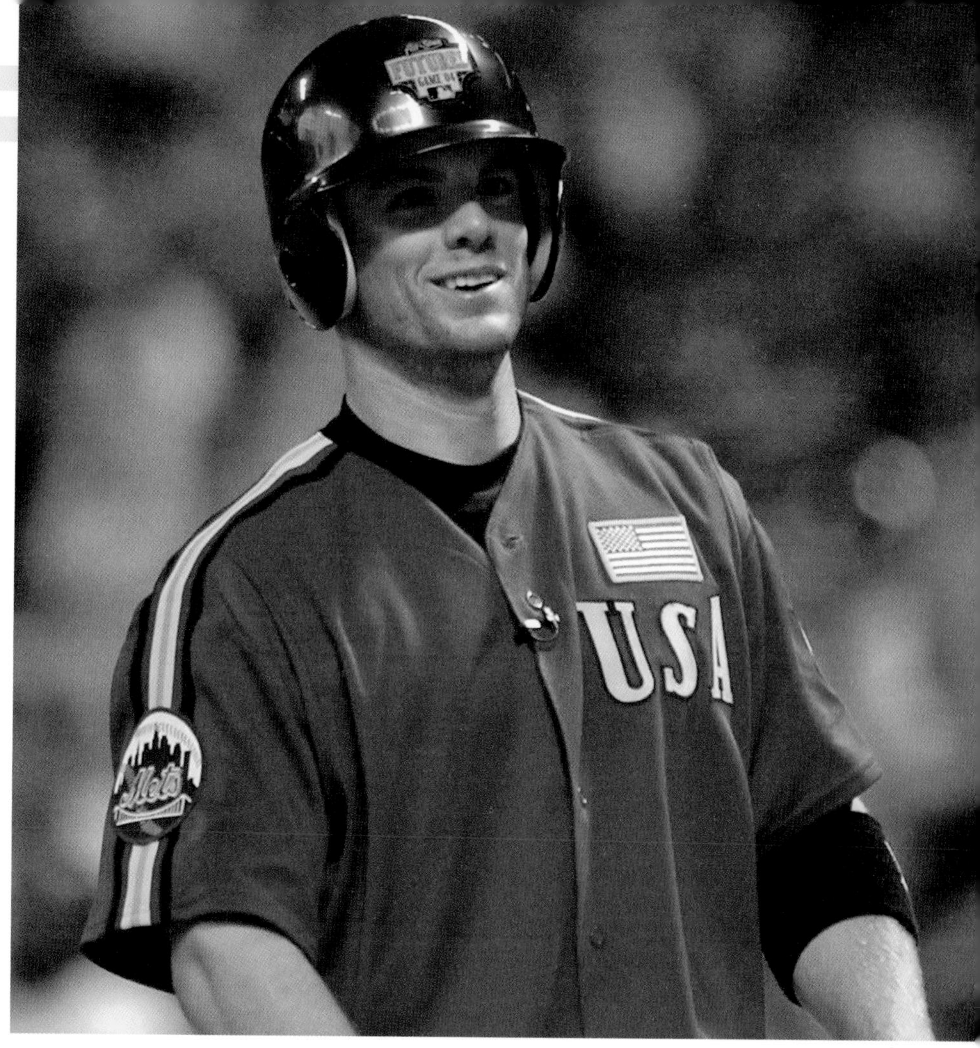

Wright competes in the All-Star Futures game twenty days before being called up to the Mets.

his own horn and declare that he was prepared to excel in the major leagues. He would allow the Mets to make that call.

It was only a matter of time. When Wright was asked about the inevitable call from the Mets, he spoke with anticipation. But he also expressed his willingness to continue working at his craft. Though he had left little doubt at Norfolk that he could handle big-league pitching, his play at third base left some wondering whether he could perform well enough in the field to warrant a promotion.

Wright was a far more natural hitter than he was a fielder, which made him work that much harder at third base. He toiled endlessly with Tides infield coordinator Edgar Alfonzo to become dependable in the field and to learn all the nuances of playing third base.

> "I've still got a lot of work to be successful. I'm not satisfied."
>
> —*David Wright*

"I'm excited of the possibility of making the jump this year," Wright said on July 20, when many believed he would be called up to the Mets in the next day or two. "But whether it's tomorrow or September, or sometime next year, I can't let myself be a part of the 'what if'

REPLACING A GREAT

It took an injury to one of the premier players in baseball to open up a roster spot on the Mets for Wright.

Wright was elevated to the major leagues when catcher Mike Piazza was placed on the fifteen-day disabled list with a sprained wrist.

Piazza played sixteen seasons in the major leagues, including eight with the Mets. He hit 427 home runs before retiring in 2007 and is considered by some as the greatest hitting catcher in baseball history.

game. I've still got a lot of work to be successful. I'm not satisfied."[3]

Wright's work ethic would never allow him to be satisfied. But ready or not, he was headed to the Big Apple. Less than a year earlier, Wright was playing Class A baseball. Now he would be facing the best pitchers in the sport.

SCOTT ROLEN GIVES A HELPING HAND

Wright needed some advice, and he got it from Scott Rolen. It could not have come from a more appropriate person. Rolen was a young third baseman—just like Wright. Rolen was barely past his teenage years when he was called up to the big leagues—just like Wright. Rolen came up with great anticipation—just like Wright. And Rolen was promoted to a major media market (Philadelphia)—just like Wright.

The Mets understood the similarities, which is why they set up a meeting between Rolen and Wright in mid-July. The veteran spoke about his experiences and provided words of wisdom. Wright soaked it in with tremendous interest.

"[Rolen] was in the same situation, called up about the same time, and played in a big city," Wright explained. "He told me not to get caught up in the expectations. A lot of expectations will be put on you, but you can't put them on yourself."[4]

That is easier said than done. Photographers and reporters surrounded Wright when he arrived in the

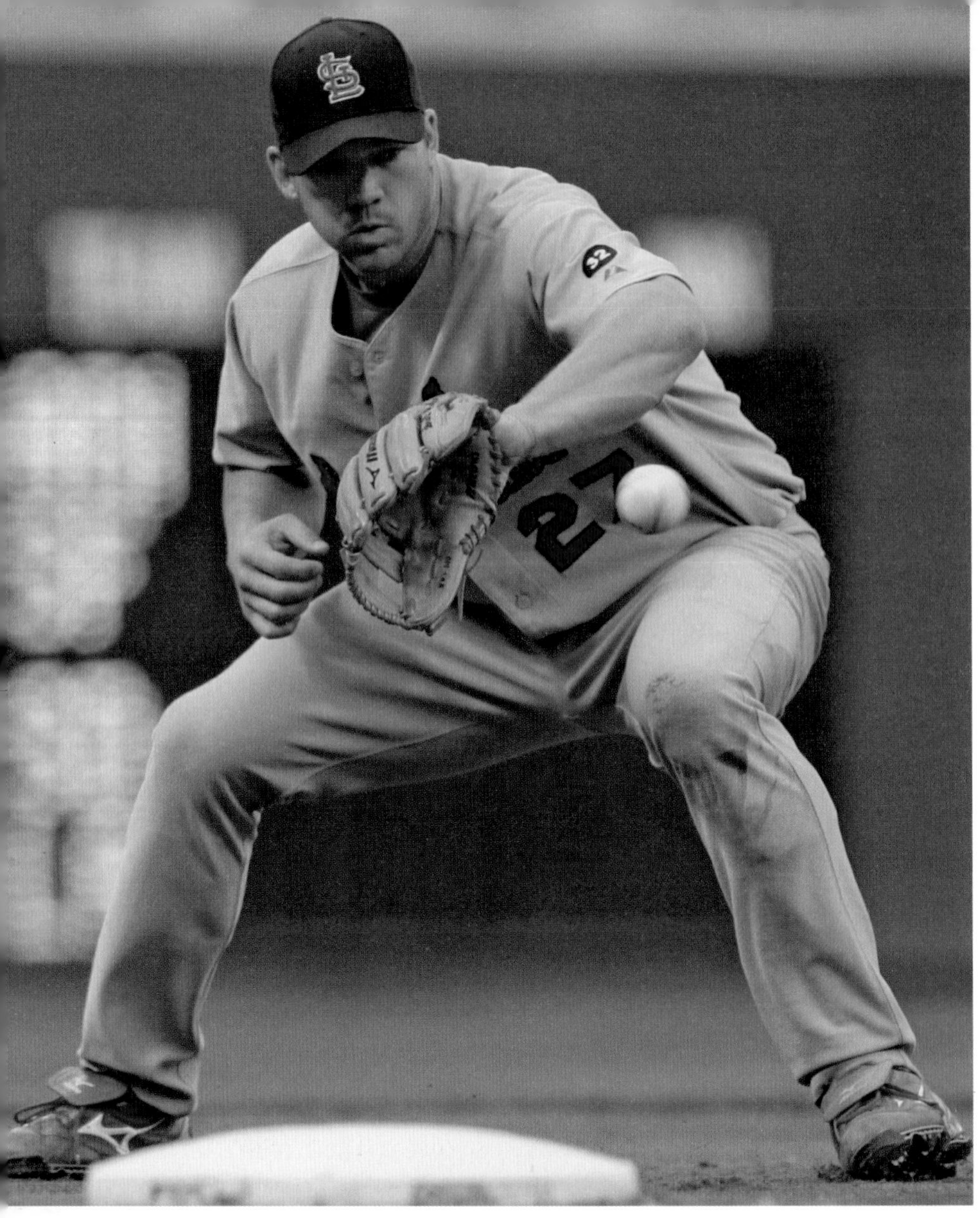

The Mets had Wright talk to veteran third baseman Scott Rolen about adjusting to the majors.

Mets clubhouse for his first major-league game on July 21. He appeared relaxed, but he later admitted that he had been so wired up that he tossed and turned in bed all night.

VIDEO GAME WIZARD

Though Wright was on the verge of becoming a baseball star, he felt no desire to stop playing video games, which was one of his favorite hobbies.

Well into his career with the Mets, he was still fiddling around with games such as "Madden College Football" and "Fight Night" on his PlayStation 3.

Wright often played such games for an hour or longer after games with the Mets. It helped him relax and get a good night's sleep.

"I could not sleep last night," he said. "Right now I'm basically just running on adrenaline."[5]

That was understandable. After all, Wright was about to make his major-league debut in the largest city in America in front of fans that saw him as their baseball savior.

David Wright was nobody's savior. But he was soon to prove that he was ready to be a baseball star.

5

EMBRACED IN THE BIG APPLE

David Wright could not help but be exhausted when he showed up at Shea Stadium for his major-league debut on July 21, 2004. After all, he had slept for a grand total of two hours the night before.

Wright, however, certainly did not act tired. In fact, he was so wired up wearing the uniform of his favorite team for the first time that he appeared jittery as the national anthem was played before the game. He shifted from one foot to the other and tapped his cap nervously against his chest.

He performed as if just as nervous, particularly at the plate. He went hitless in four at-bats and failed

Wright watches a two-run home run against the Marlins in 2008.

Wright's first major-league hit came in his second game with the Mets.

to execute a bunt, but displayed his selfless attitude by celebrating with his teammates and expressing joy after the 5–4 victory over the Montreal Expos. When asked about his performance, his answers indicated that his work ethic was not about to change now that he had reached the big leagues.

"Everything played out like it did in my dreams," Wright said. "Now I'll go back to my hotel room and soak in it, replay each at-bat and each ground ball.

"I felt overaggressive at the plate," he added. "I think it was just nerves. I was a little out of my element tonight."[1]

ADJUSTING TO THE BIG LEAGUES

He would be out of his element for a while. Wright batted a weak .192 in his first seven games with the Mets. During one game, he came to the plate with runners on first and third and nobody out. But rather than wait for a pitch he could handle, he swung at a tough slider at the knees and grounded out.

Teammate Mike Piazza wandered over to an upset Wright in the dugout, put his arm around his shoulder, and suggested nicely that he wait for pitches he wanted to swing at rather than helping pitchers out by being impatient. Soon Mets hitting coach Don Baylor added his belief that Wright was a bit intimidated by major-league pitchers.

After that slow start, however, Wright heated up with the weather. He became sizzling hot during a sweltering August. He elevated his batting average to

MAN'S BEST FRIEND

Even after Wright became a Major League Baseball star, he still called home often.

He was not just checking on his parents and siblings though. Wright also wanted to know how his dog, Homer, was doing.

Homer, which would seem to be a perfect name for the dog of a baseball player, is a boxer.

Mets catcher Mike Piazza helped Wright adjust to Major League pitching.

a respectable .261 with 4 home runs and 13 runs batted in by the middle of the month. It was quite remarkable considering Wright was toiling in Class A just a year earlier.

On one occasion, Mets catcher Vance Wilson suggested to Wright that he become more aggressive at the plate. Though Wright had raised his average, he was still hitting too many weak singles. Wilson wanted Wright to begin showing the power he had displayed in the minor leagues. In his next at-bat, Wright smashed a 455-foot home run to left field. When he rounded third base, Wright looked into the dugout and winked at Wilson.

TAKING IT ALL IN

Wright acted like a student with teachers all around him. He studied Piazza, whom many considered the premier hitting catcher in the history of baseball. Wright watched how Piazza stared at tapes of opposing pitchers, learning every nuance of their deliveries to the plate and soaking in their strengths and weaknesses.

He understood that Piazza's success was not based strictly on talent. Piazza worked at his craft, a fact that cemented Wright's own belief that he had to continue to do the same.

His teammates certainly noticed. Infielder Joe McEwing marveled at Wright's work ethic and

DON'T TURN UP THE HEAT

One of Wright's most unusual thrills occurred when his likeness was made into a wax figure.

Wright was featured in Madame Tussauds, a New York wax museum featuring some of the most prominent people to ever live or work in that city. The unveiling of the Wright wax figure brought out a huge crowd of Mets fans.

Also unveiled at the same time was a wax figure of popular New York Yankees shortstop Derek Jeter.

BIG LEAGUE CHEWER!

One of the achievements that made Wright proud had nothing to do with baseball.

It was when he won a bubblegum blowing contest for charity.

Wright blew a fourteen-inch bubble and then expressed his feeling of pride at accomplishing the feat.

curiosity, not just about baseball, but everything regarding the life of a major-league player. "He's very inquisitive; it's refreshing," McEwing said. "David wants to know everything about being a big leaguer, including things like how to [leave a tip at a restaurant]."[2]

> "David wants to know everything about being a big leaguer."
>
> —Joe McEwing

By late August, Mets manager Art Howe admitted that the twenty-one-year-old Wright was already among the team's premier hitters. He elevated Wright to the third spot in the batting order, which is generally reserved for the best all-around hitter on a team.

But rather than shrink from the responsibility, Wright ran with it. By mid-September, his batting average had climbed to .300 and he had already belted 10 home runs. He and young shortstop

Jose Reyes had become the shining lights in a dismal season for the Mets. They were the future of a team that was old and struggling.

Wright finished 2004 with a strong .293 batting average, which tied St. Louis Cardinals second baseman Aaron Miles for the highest among National League rookies that season. Wright also contributed 14 home runs and 40 runs batted in. He was named to the Baseball America All-Rookie team, which is remarkable considering he played less than half a season.

But Wright wanted consistency, which he did not achieve as a rookie in New York. He felt content about the games in which he drove in 6 runs against Milwaukee, slammed 2 home runs against Florida and collected 4 hits against San Francisco.

A DIFFERENT KIND OF STRIKE

Wright has been an avid bowler throughout his life. In fact, he has always brought his own bowling shoes rather than renting a pair at the lanes.

Why? Because he's a bit squeamish about germs.

"It's for hygiene purposes more than anything," he said. "I'm not a hygiene freak or anything. I'm just not so into wearing other people's shoes and sticking my fingers in things that strangers have touched."

He even managed two streaks in which he recorded at least one hit in seven consecutive games. But he also suffered through long dry spells in which he would manage just a few singles over the course of a week.

Despite the ups and downs, it had been a highly encouraging first year in the major leagues for Wright. And he would take the momentum and run with it.

Many second-year players who had performed well as rookies fall victim to what is known as the "Sophomore Slump." But Wright showed immediately that he was not going to be among them. He cracked a grand slam against archrival Philadelphia two weeks into the 2005 season and hit safely in nine consecutive games, batting an impressive .448 during that stretch.

Wright was just warming up. He continued smashing the ball, adding an eight-game hitting

NEW YORK'S NEW HEARTTHROB

One teammate who joked about all the young women and teenage girls who swooned over Wright was infielder Chris Woodward.

"I mean, he's OK looking, but it's not like he's Brad Pitt," Woodward exclaimed.

streak in May, during which he batted a mind-boggling .571.

A BONA FIDE SUPERSTAR

David Wright was no longer a star-in-waiting. He was a star. That became apparent on July 14.

It was quite an emotional evening for Wright. Before the game, he met Sarah Hughes, the 2002 Olympic gold medal winner in figure skating. He admitted to the media that the experience was a thrill because he loved the Olympics and got choked up when the national anthem was played after an American won a gold medal.

Wright also showed his heart that night to a high school friend named Jessica Yantz, who had already appeared on the popular TV show *American Idol* and was looking to break into show business as a singer. Yantz asked Wright to help her land the job of singing the national anthem before a Mets game.

He indeed arranged it, and then watched with pride as Yantz belted out the song on that night of July 14. When she finished, Wright gave her his own personal standing ovation.

The thrills had just begun. Wright slammed a pair of home runs in that game and made a brilliant play at third base in the eighth inning. He sped for a popup hit by Atlanta's Kelly Johnson, then lunged for it. Wright snagged the ball just before it hit the ground.

Stunned base runner Andy Marte did not believe there was any chance Wright could catch the ball, so he had already raced from third to home. Wright simply jogged over to third base and touched the bag for a double play that helped the Mets win.

It was a tremendous performance by Wright. Even his 16th error of the season could not wreck one of the best evenings of his young career. To make matters even sweeter, the victory propelled the Mets to within a half-game of the last playoff spot in the National League.

"Kind of a whirlwind of emotions," expressed Wright about his feelings after the game. "I keep telling people I'm going to learn something from [the errors]. I really think I am. Making those errors, it's going to help me."[3]

Wright was just as interested in what was going to help others as he was in what was going to help himself. He would soon show the world that he did not just use his heart on the field.

6

MORE THAN A BASEBALL STAR

It was no secret from the time he began swinging a bat in Little League that David Wright could hit a baseball.

He could hit it hard and he could hit it far. In his childhood, adolescence, and adulthood, he made pitchers cringe every time he stepped to the plate.

But Wright wanted to be known as more than just a great hitter. He yearned to earn a reputation as a sure-handed third baseman as well. Fielding did not come as naturally to him as smashing a baseball with a bat.

Third base is known as the "hot corner" because when right-handed batters pull the ball, it comes off the bat with great velocity. Those hits often head right to the third baseman.

Wright understood that he had more quickness in his hands and wrists, which are used to swing the bat, than he had in his feet, which are needed to reach hard-hit ground balls. But nobody had to tell him to work harder on his fielding. And by the second half of the 2005 season, he had become far more proficient at third base.

MASTERING THE FIELD

That became apparent in the seventh inning of a game against San Diego in early August, when Wright made what some believed to be the play of the year in Major League Baseball. Padres slugger Brian Giles lofted the ball toward left field and Wright sprinted after it and dove with every ounce of strength he had in his legs. He reached out his arm as he descended to the ground and caught the ball barehanded.

It is not often a crowd in another city will give a player from an opposing team a standing ovation, but Wright received one that night in San Diego.

Mets first baseman Doug Mientkiewicz was flabbergasted, telling reporters that he choked on a sunflower seed when he witnessed Wright's feat. He believed that cable sports channel ESPN should recognize the play in the annual award ceremonies called the ESPYs. "If that's not the Play of the Year, I'll protest," Mientkiewicz said.[1]

IN THE CLUTCH

The most opportune time for a batter to come to the plate is with the bases loaded, which occurs when there is a runner at each base.

Wright thrived in those situations in 2005, getting 7 hits in 13 at-bats with 2 home runs, 4 doubles, and 21 RBIs. That means he recorded more than one-fifth of his RBIs for the season with the bases loaded.

And, in fact, long-time baseball highlight show This Week in Baseball did select Wright's catch as its Play of the Year.

The modest Wright told teammate Mike Cameron that he was just lucky. But even Wright could not claim luck the next night, when he slammed a three-run home run, two-run double, and RBI single to give the Mets a 9–1 victory over the Padres.

A MASTER SLUGGER, TOO

By that time, even though Wright had only been playing Major League Baseball for just over a year, Mets manager Willie Randolph was already comparing his potential to that of Hall of Fame third basemen such as George Brett, Wade Boggs, and Mike Schmidt.

Mets

Wright's hard work paid off, as he developed into a great fielder.

Wright was showing more than just potential in the second half of the 2005 season. He belted 2 home runs in one game during a series against Arizona in which he reached base in nine consecutive at-bats. He was the first Mets player to accomplish that feat in five years.

Still just twenty-two years old, Wright was recognized as the National League Player of the Week soon thereafter. And while he was improving on defense, he was displaying incredible versatility offensively. He embarked on an eleven-game hitting streak in late August in which he batted .432 with 13 runs scored, 3 doubles, 4 home runs, and even 3 stolen bases.

Most power hitters are rather slow afoot and cannot consistently steal bases. Most speed merchants

NO WEAKNESS

More than a year after Wright burst upon the scene with the Mets, the top pitchers in the National League were still scratching their heads over how to get him out.

Among them was right-hander John Smoltz, who pitched for more than twenty years for the Atlanta Braves and was among the few pitchers in baseball history to record more than 3,000 strikeouts.

"I wish I knew how to pitch that kid," said Smoltz. "As hard as it is to fathom, he doesn't have a weakness."

Ramon Castro congratulates Wright after a grand slam against the Washington Nationals.

who do steal bases rarely hit home runs. Wright, however, could do both. He was becoming one of the premier all-around offensive threats in the game.

Wright proved to be among the best hitters in baseball after the midseason break, during which the top players in the National League and American League compete in the annual All-Star Game.

From that time forward, Wright batted an exceptional .333 and he finished the season with a .306

THE SECOND BEST

Only one player in baseball—and none in the National League—bested Wright in all the major statistical categories in 2005.

That player was New York Yankees star Alex Rodriguez. Rodriguez was the lone player who finished the season with a higher batting average and more home runs, runs batted in, and stolen bases.

average, eighth-best in the National League. He added 27 home runs and became the first Met in five years to exceed 100 runs batted in. Wright was even second on the team with 17 stolen bases.

STAYING GROUNDED

But there is more to success in life than success in baseball, especially in New York. Wright understood from the moment he stepped foot in the city known as The Big Apple that there would be plenty of potential distractions. New York is known for its parties and nightlife. And as a high-profile athlete, he was the target of people who wanted a piece of his time and money and could not be trusted.

It is not that Wright did not enjoy the fine cultural events and restaurants in New York. He also made new friends. But he was careful about the people he spent time with. And he loved his old friends enough that he had no desire to abandon them just because he had become rich and famous.

Wright attributed that mindset to being the son of a police officer. He valued the lessons he learned growing up about what was really important and meaningful in life. Those values included hard work and lasting friendships. He did not want anything to distract him from becoming the best baseball player he could possibly be.

"I'm really careful about making friends, about who I surround myself with," Wright said. "Most of my friends are people I've known since I was a kid. . . . I just make sure I'm around people I can trust."[2]

Wright certainly trusted the Mets after the 2005 season when they decided simply to renew his contract at $374,000 a year, which was barely above the minimum salary teams are allowed to play their players. He was hoping that his achievements would motivate the Mets to offer a lucrative, long-term deal, but he was not the type of player to complain.

FOOTBALL FANDOM

Though David joined his father Rhon as an avid Mets fan during his childhood, their rooting interests in football went different directions.

As are most Virginians, Rhon was a fan of the Washington Redskins, which is the team located closest to the area. But David adopted the archrival New York Giants as his favorite NFL team.

"I did not agree, but that's life," he said. "I make a lot more money than both my parents combined, so, in my mind, I've got it pretty good. How many other twenty-three-year-olds get to play a game for a living and act like a kid? The worst day on a ball field is better than the best day in any office.

"I've got it pretty good. . . . The worst day on a ball field is better than the best day in any office."

—David Wright

"I refuse to have a bitter taste in my mouth about this game. As soon as baseball becomes a job, as soon as I stop caring, as soon as the smile goes away, I'll hang up my spikes and do something else."[3]

THE DAVID WRIGHT FOUNDATION

Wright was not about to stop caring—about baseball or those less fortunate than him. That is why he

ROOKIE INITATION

One duty of rookies in Major League Baseball is that they often must do favors for veteran teammates.

Wright was no exception. He always carried the luggage for outfielder Cliff Floyd in airports and hotels.

Floyd, who enjoyed arguably his finest season in 2005 with the Mets, became one of Wright's mentors and closest friends.

began the David Wright Foundation after the 2005 season. He became most involved in the fight against multiple sclerosis, a disease that attacks the central nervous system consisting of the brain, spinal cord, and optic nerves. It can lead to numbness or even paralysis and blindness.

The David Wright Foundation was launched on December 14, 2005, in a benefit held at the prestigious New York Stock Exchange Members Club. More than $100,000 was raised for various multiple sclerosis centers in the city.

That was only the beginning. In the years to follow, Wright would become one of the most charitable athletes in the world.

7 DOING THE "WRIGHT" THING

It has been said that wealth and fame are only meaningful if they are used to help others. Otherwise they are only valuable to the person who has achieved them.

Those who know David Wright believe that his wealth and fame have been used to make life better for the sick or underprivileged. But they also feel that his motivation for helping others comes from the heart rather than as a means to focus attention on himself.

David Wright threw his first pitch for the battle against multiple sclerosis at the first "Do the Wright Thing" banquet a little more than a week before Christmas in 2005. Among the contributors were major-league stars such as Scott Rolen, Cliff Floyd, Dontrelle Willis, Todd Zeile, Jason Marquis, and 2002 Olympic gold medalist Sarah Hughes.

Wright was motivated to choose multiple sclerosis as his pet project when he learned that the wife of friend and agent Keith Miller was one of hundreds of thousands of Americans stricken with the disease.

New York Yankees shortstop Derek Jeter, who was arguably the most popular athlete in the city, launched his Turn 2 Foundation during his rookie season. Wright noted the success of Jeter's charitable work and yearned to follow in the same footsteps.

"It's something I wanted to do since I started playing baseball," Wright said. "You see players making impacts with their foundations. I wanted to be a part of that."[1]

THERE FOR A FRIEND

Wright received an emotional reaction from agent Keith Miller when informed that his client chose multiple sclerosis as his pet charity because Miller's wife was stricken with the disease.

Miller, a former major-league infielder, was moved by Wright's actions.

"He doesn't usually get so emotional," Wright said. "But I talked to him a couple of times on the phone and you could tell he was tearing up a little bit."

Wright remembers getting autographs as a kid and tries to sign as many as he can.

JUST GETTING STARTED

Wright was just getting started. Though the fight against multiple sclerosis remained a primary focus, the David Wright Foundation greatly expanded its scope over the next few years. Among the organizations it benefited were the Make-A-Wish Foundation of New York, for children with life-threatening illnesses, and the Toys for Tots campaign, which raises money to provide toys for children whose families cannot afford them.

The respect and love he felt for his father, who worked as a police officer in Virginia, motivated Wright to become involved with the Police Athletic League, which benefits underprivileged youth.

He also raised money for the Patrolmen's Benevolent Association.

The notion of living and playing in New York overwhelms some athletes, but Wright used it to his advantage. Not only did he get recognized more for his baseball talents in the nation's largest city, but it also afforded him the opportunity to maximize his charitable work.

"I understand that I'm very fortunate to be in the position I'm in, where I can use my name to influence the community," he said. "If I can use my name to influence people in a positive light, then that's something that's well worth it.

"I realize that I'm young and I've only been here a couple years, but New York's a great place to play baseball. The community really rallies around our players, so I've been able to use that to my advantage and the advantage of our foundation."[2]

NO. 5 IS NO. 1

Popularity in the world of sports can often be judged by how many jerseys and other items are sold with a particular player's name on them.

How popular had Wright become in 2006 in New York, New Jersey, and Connecticut?

Very popular. In that year, his No. 5 jersey outsold the No. 2 jersey of immensely popular New York Yankees shortstop Derek Jeter in those states.

HELPING THE CHILDREN

By the middle of 2006, the David Wright Foundation was gearing itself more toward charities to benefit children. It launched the first Kids Event at a New York bowling center in late August for widows and their kids who lost fathers during the September 11, 2001, terrorist attack that destroyed the World Trade Centers in that city.

The foundation lured a wide-ranging variety of celebrities to the event, including Hughes, actor and comedian Mike Myers, Mets general manager Omar Minaya, and actress Rosie Perez.

Wright particularly enjoyed the festivities as an avid bowler himself, but watching the children who had suffered through such a tragedy in their lives laugh and frolic on the lanes made the experience even more fun for him. The kids left that day with a bagful of prizes, including two tickets to a Mets game.

STAR SUPPORT

As the years progressed, the more famous the guests became at Wright's charitable events.

At the 2006 "Do the Wright Thing Gala" held four weeks before Christmas, the guests included popular pop singer Nick Lachey.

Lachey performed several songs at the event, including a few from the album *What's Left of Me* as well as others from his days with the group 98 Degrees.

Wright dressed as Santa Claus and handed out gifts to children at the Mets' annual holiday party in 2006.

The David Wright Foundation continued to raise money for the battle against multiple sclerosis, but its founder was branching out in his charitable endeavors. In early 2007, he held a baseball camp to benefit the White Plains Hospital Center. The proceeds helped fund an emergency center at the hospital dedicated exclusively to sick children.

Kids who attended the event learned about batting, pitching, fielding, and base running from

HELP FROM THE TEAM

Though Wright organized the baseball clinic to support the White Plains Hospital Center in January 2007, he received plenty of help from teammates and former Mets during the event.

Among those attending was budding superstar shortstop Jose Reyes, whom the Mets planned on teaming up with Wright on the left side of the infield for years to come.

Also at the clinic were current Mets such as Paul Lo Duca, Orlando Hernandez, and John Maine, as well as former Mets stars Lee Mazzilli and Howard Johnson.

Wright and his teammates. They then asked the players questions, joined them in a photo session, and received their autographs.

Working with children and with children's hospitals gave Wright his greatest satisfaction. After visiting young multiple sclerosis patients at Holy Name Hospital in Teaneck, New Jersey, he was not certain who enjoyed the experience more.

"I think I ended up getting more out of it than the patients did," he said. "It was an amazing experience and it made me want to do more."[3]

So he did more. During the first three years of its existence, the David Wright Foundation worked with organizations such as the Boys and Girls Clubs, Kids in Crisis, Fresh Air Fund, Tuesday's Children, Harlem Children's Zone, Children's Village, and the New York University Hospital Neonatal Intensive Care Unit. All of them were geared toward kids.

One of the goals of the foundation was to give underprivileged and poor children the opportunity to escape their environments, if only for one day. In May 2007, it teamed up with the Mets Foundation to launch the 5 Star*Kids program, which provided tickets to Mets games to kids involved in various youth organizations.

Another night out at Shea Stadium was sponsored by the Patrolmen's Benevolent Association, which was particularly close to Wright's heart.

"I am in a position where I can bring these kids to the ballpark to enjoy a game," Wright said. "The PBA is especially important to me because my father, Rhon, is a police officer in Virginia and I can identify with the issues and emotions that come with being an officer's child. My goal is to provide these kids with a positive, long-lasting memory."[4]

THE VIRGINIA TECH TRAGEDY

Not all of Wright's charitable work was planned in advance. One particular event was the result of a tragedy that struck suddenly, unexpectedly, and hit very close to home. On April 16, 2007, a troubled pupil at Virginia Tech University killed thirty-two students and teachers before turning the gun on himself.

Wright knew that his brother Stephen was an engineering student at the school, which sent him into a panic. After all, some of the shootings took place at the engineering school.

"My heart definitely skipped a couple of beats when I heard that the engineering building was one of the shooting sites," Wright recalled. "But I talked to my brother Matthew and found out that Stephen was safe. That eased my mind, but I could not help feeling sorry for the victims and their families. That whole area is home to me and I knew that I needed to do something."[5]

> **"That whole area is home to me and I knew that I needed to do something."**
>
> *—David Wright*

Wright certainly did something. He teamed up with Maroon Effect, a group of Virginia Tech alumni living in the New York area, to raise funds for the families of the shooting victims. He also established an annual scholarship at the school that provided four years of tuition for an engineering student.

He knew, however, that only production on the baseball field would allow him to continue making the world a better place for others, especially children. Wright was off to a brilliant start, but other major-

STILL YOUNG

Wright often joked with Mets pitcher Tom Glavine about the differences in their ages.

During one exchange, Wright said to the forty-one-year-old Glavine, "Hey, man, I was a huge fan of yours when I was in elementary school." Glavine replied, "Look, you'll be lucky if you're still playing at my age, and you won't look as good as I do."

Glavine was in the midst of a brilliant career in which he won more than 300 games.

league players had performed well early in their careers, only to tail off.

Wright understood that wealth and fame were two necessary ingredients in maximizing charitable efforts. And in 2006, both his wealth and fame were to grow even more.

8 ACHIEVING A DREAM FOR TEAM

An old expression to describe a woman who is searching for the perfect man is that she is "looking for Mr. Right."

Well, in 2006, many were looking for Mr. Wright.

"David Wright, I love you!" shouted one teenage girl before an early 2006 game at Shea Stadium.

Her friend echoed that sentiment: "I love you, David Wright," she screamed. "Will you marry us?"[1]

Soon shirts were being printed and worn by hundreds of female fans that read "MRS. WRIGHT" in large bold lettering. And Wright was receiving hundreds of marriage proposals.

Wright quickly became a fan favorite with the New York Mets.

Such attention might have proven quite a distraction to a typical player, but Wright was no typical player. He had been driven to maximize his potential from the moment he began swinging a bat as a child and nothing was going to deter him heading into the 2006 season. After all, Wright had still never played on the National League All-Star team, nor had he helped the Mets qualify for the playoffs.

It is not that Wright shied away from publicity. He signed endorsement deals with Vitamin Water, Wilson, and Delta Airlines, which named one of its

SEINFELD

One celebrity Wright met in 2006 was comedian Jerry Seinfeld, whose 1990s TV sitcom based in New York was among the most successful in history.

One day during the season, Seinfeld appeared at batting practice before a game. Wright spent the next several minutes laughing at Seinfeld's jokes and giving the comedian a few points on the art of hitting.

planes "The Wright Flight." He was featured on the cover of the PlayStation game MLB 07. He landed a spot as a guest on *The Late Show with David Letterman*. He was even invited to the White House to have dinner with President George W. Bush.

A HOT START

But Wright had his priorities and was ready to roll from the first pitch of the season. He slammed at least one hit in each of the first eight games in 2006. But, more importantly, he was tremendously productive, smashing 3 home runs, scoring 9 runs, and driving in 12 more during that stretch.

The Mets were also finding out what every teammate of Wright had learned since he was a Little Leaguer. That is, he was very dependable. Wright played every inning in each of the first forty-six games of the 2006 season.

And he continued to belt the baseball, slamming out 4 hits in a game three times in May and hitting a home run in three consecutive games twice during a three-week period in May and June. A week later, he belted 2 home runs in a game against Cincinnati.

The fans, players, managers, and media members certainly noticed. The result of Wright's late spring and early summer explosion was that he was named National League Player of the Month in June, during which he recorded a .327 batting average with 20 runs, 10 home runs, 29 RBIs, and 3 stolen bases.

Wright was also picked to represent the National League as the starting third baseman in the annual All-Star Game against the American League. Wright received both honors for the first time in his career.

THE ALL-STAR GAME

The National League was in the midst of a long losing streak in the midsummer classic and 2006 was no exception. The American League won the game played at beautiful PNC Park in Pittsburgh, 3–2, but Wright was ready for the national spotlight. He not only became only the second Mets player in history to clout a home run in the annual AL–NL showdown, but the first in major-league history to hit one in his first All-Star Game at-bat.

Wright also participated in the Century 21 Home Run Derby, which featured four power hitters from each league competing against one another. And he

Wright and Phillies slugger Ryan Howard topped the Home Run Derby at the 2006 All-Star Game.

nearly won the event, which took place the night before the All-Star Game. He placed second to Philadelphia slugger Ryan Howard.

Wright had been receiving tremendous attention in New York, but not beyond. The national media began to take notice after his brilliant performance

FOLLOWING A GREAT

Wright was the second Met to hit a home run in the annual All-Star Game.

Who was the first? It was outfielder Lee Mazzilli, who slugged one in 1979, which proved to be his only All-Star Game appearance.

Mazzilli was very popular with Mets fans because he was born and raised in New York. He began his major-league career with the Mets, then returned to them for his last three years in baseball. Mazzilli also spent a short time with the New York Yankees.

through the first three months of the 2006 season and his heroics during the all-star break. He was particularly thrilled at the invitation to appear on *The Late Show with David Letterman*, a talk show taped in New York that had been a staple of late-night television in America since 1982.

"I'm such a big fan of [Letterman]," Wright said. "I could not believe I was there."[2]

It has been said that the baseball season is a marathon rather than a sprint. Many players simply cannot keep up the pace after a sensational first half, but Wright was not among them. He batted over .300 from mid-July to mid-August before finally slumping for a couple weeks.

MR. INDEPENDENT

Wright's fame spread during and after the 2006 season. Among the publications that sent a reporter to interview him was the women's magazine *Cosmopolitan*.

When asked if the single Wright had any turn-offs on a date, he answered that he was an independent guy who appreciated the same trait in a woman. And he added that finding the ideal woman to marry was not his first priority in life at that time.

"My biggest deal-breaker is a girl who's clingy," he said. "So far serious relationships for me have been few and far between. Right now, everything in my life comes second to baseball."

MAKING A COMMITMENT

By that time, Wright had become a very wealthy man. In early August, the Mets signed him to a six-year contract worth $55 million. They rewarded him not only for his performance on the field, but his connection with the fans that would lead to more money coming in to the Mets organization.

And Wright was ecstatic.

"I have wanted to be a life-long Met and this is the first step in that direction," he said. "It's a special feeling to be drafted by my favorite team. To know I'm going to be a Met for the next six or seven years is going to be special."[3]

Wright again showed his selflessness and generosity by announcing he would donate $1.5 million of his pay to the Mets' charitable foundation.

He then heated up down the stretch, collecting at least 2 hits in nine of the last fourteen games of the regular season. He embarked on a twelve-game hitting streak, batting .362 with 2 home runs during that stretch.

Wright finished ninth in the National League with a .311 batting average and tied for seventh with 116 RBIs. He displayed an ability to hit under pressure, placing sixth in the league with a .365 batting average with runners on second or third base. He also became the fourth player in Mets history to rack up 100 RBIs or more in consecutive seasons.

PLAYOFF BOUND

More importantly to Wright, the Mets had finally become a champion. They took over first place in the

A LETHAL LEFT SIDE

Wright signed his six-year contract in 2006 just three days after Mets shortstop Jose Reyes agreed to a four-year deal worth more than $23 million.

That locked up the left side of the Mets infield through 2010.

Reyes was also in the midst of a brilliant 2006 season when he signed his contract. He batted .300 with 19 home runs and 81 RBIs that year and led the National League with 64 stolen bases. He too landed a spot on the National League All-Star team that year.

Wright (top) celebrates as the Mets reach the postseason for the first time since 2000.

National League East in the second game of the year and remained in front the rest of the way. In fact, they clinched the division championship with more than two weeks left in the season. And that earned them a chance to play for a spot in the World Series.

Wright was ready. He smacked 2 doubles and drove in 3 runs in the first playoff game of his career to lead the Mets to a 6-5 victory over Los Angeles.

HOME SWEET HOME

Wright could certainly afford a good home in New York City once he signed the $55 million contract with the Mets.

He shopped around before buying a 4,000-square-foot penthouse loft in the borough of Manhattan. The apartment is in what is known as the Flatiron District of New York, which houses the Empire State Building and is known for its expensive restaurants.

The asking price for the apartment Wright purchased was $6.5 million.

He added another hit and RBI three days later in a 9–5 victory that clinched a three-game sweep of the Dodgers. The Mets trailed 5–4 in that game before rallying to victory.

"We've been doing that all year," Wright said after the game. "We're a resilient team. It seems when we get down, it pushes us, motivates us more to take the lead."[4]

> **"We're a resilient team. It seems when we get down, it pushes us . . . "**
>
> *—David Wright*

Motivation would be no problem in the showdown against St. Louis for the

National League title, but hitting the ball would. The Mets scored either one or zero runs in three of their four losses and were eliminated. Wright struggled along with the rest of his teammates, managing just 4 hits in 25 at-bats against the Cardinals, though he did club his first postseason home run in a 12–5 victory in Game 4.

Wright was devastated, especially since his team had come within one victory of qualifying for the Series, but at just twenty-three years old, he believed that there would be many more chances to lead his team to a championship.

In fact, one such opportunity was just over the horizon.

9

GREAT SEASON, SAD ENDING

Major-league pitchers are smart. And they exchange notes. It takes a while to learn the weaknesses of opposing hitters, but once pitchers do find those weaknesses, they exploit them. And they attack them.

The problem for pitchers when they faced Wright? They could not find any weaknesses.

They pitched him outside and he would hit a double to right field. They pitched him inside and he would yank the ball over the fence. They pitched him low and he would golf the ball for a home run. They pitched him high and he would just let it go by. Wright displayed a level swing and an amazing combination of aggressiveness and patience at the plate.

The premier baseball players are sometimes called "naturals" because they seem to have been born to achieve greatness. Wright never considered himself to be in that category. He understood that he had to work hard for everything he achieved on a baseball field.

That work ethic served him well from his Little League days, allowing him to ascend to the professional level, reach the major leagues quickly, and become a star at age twenty-three. And that took desire. Wright yearned to excel in every aspect of the game. And though he still struggled a bit at third base, by 2006 he had improved in the field as well.

"I want to hit for power, hit for average, steal bases, play good defense, make throws," he said. "There are so many players out there who are better than me talent-wise. But I like to think I'll outwork all of them."[1]

A DIFFERENT KIND OF PLAYER

Some offered that Wright's attitudes toward baseball and life were a throwback to another era. They believed that the millions of dollars earned by players in his generation made them less likely to work hard once they signed a big contract. And they also believed that that financial wealth negatively changed their personalities.

Those same critics felt Wright was different. Not only did he continue to work tirelessly to improve, but he also interacted with others the same way he did at Hickory High School five years earlier. There was not a trace of cockiness or arrogance in him.

"He comes across as so wholesome that you suspect he was [scientifically] frozen sometime around 1955 and thawed out three years ago, when he made his first start at third base in the major leagues," wrote David Amsden of *New York* magazine. "His friends note, almost apologetically, that he is unwaveringly polite and humble, and even those who hate him admit that . . . actually, scratch that. No one hates David Wright."[2]

"He comes across as so wholesome that you suspect he was [scientifically] frozen sometime around 1955 and thawed out three years ago . . ."

—David Amsden

Opposing pitchers might. They were especially not happy with him early in the 2007 season. Wright opened the year on fire at the plate, reaching base

EATING WELL

Athletes who love a wide variety of food are fortunate to play in New York.

Wright has been no exception. He told *New York Times* reporter Michael S. Schmidt in early 2007 that his favorite restaurants were Smith & Wollensky and Tao. The former is a steakhouse while the latter features Asian cuisine.

A GOOD SPORT

Early in the 2007 season, a waitress handed Wright a napkin, which she wanted him to sign.

"Will you sign this even though I'm a [St. Louis] Cardinals fan?" she asked.

Wright pretended he was offended. After all, the Cardinals had beaten his Mets in the 2006 National League Championship Series. He smiled and wrote the following words on the napkin:

"To my favorite Cardinals fan, the Mets rule!!! David Wright."

safely in the first twenty-three games, the third longest such streak in Mets history. He also opened the year with at least one hit in each of the first fourteen games, establishing a new franchise record.

Wright hit no home runs in April, but certainly made up for it in May by sending 8 over the fence. He was merely warming up. He belted a home run in four consecutive games in early June, when he was in the midst of a seventeen-game hitting streak. He also stole 19 consecutive bases without being caught.

Wright was headed for San Francisco, not for a game against the Giants, but for his second consecutive All-Star Game appearance. The National League lost again, but Wright started at third base and collected one hit.

And if folks believed Wright was hot before the all-star break, they had not seen anything yet. He drove in at least one run in six consecutive games in mid-July, slammed 4 hits in one game against Milwaukee on August 2, then rocketed 2 home runs nine days later against Florida.

By that time, many pitchers decided they wanted no part of David Wright. They began pitching around him and taking their chances with other Mets batters. Wright walked 4 times in one game against San Diego after having walked at least once in ten consecutive games earlier in the season.

MELTDOWN

All appeared well for Wright and the Mets. The team grabbed first place in the National League East in mid-May and strengthened its hold on it for the next

PARTNERS IN CRIME

Both Wright and Mets shortstop Jose Reyes stole 30 bases in 2006 and 2007.

And they made history by doing it.

The pair became the second teammates in ninety-three years to achieve that feat in the same season. The others were Cincinnati's Barry Larkin and Chris Sabo, who did it in 1988.

GETTING NOTICED

When you impress the man who is commonly believed to be the best player in baseball, you have certainly accomplished something.

Following the 2006 season, New York Yankees slugger Alex Rodriguez expressed his admiration for Wright.

"It looks like he has a real good idea of the game, a real respect for the game," said the superstar known as 'A-Rod'. "That's rare for young players to have that type of feel at the plate and for the game. He has an outstanding reputation as a player, and it's well deserved."

four months. By September 12, they were seven games ahead of second-place Philadelphia. Another division championship seemed a certainty. After all, no team in the history of baseball had ever lost such a big lead that late in the season.

But suddenly the Mets started to crumble. They lost three straight to surging Philadelphia and two of three to the weak Washington Nationals before rebounding to win three of four against Florida. The Mets then lost five in a row to fall out of first place. And after a loss to Florida on September 28, Wright challenged his teammates to rise up.

Though just twenty-four years old, Wright was in his fourth year with the team and considered himself

After a bright start, the Mets' 2008 season ended in disappointment.

a leader. He was angry and frustrated that everything the team had worked for since the start of spring training in February was slipping away. And he let everyone know about it.

"Personally, I'm embarrassed," he said. "It's pretty pathetic that we have this division within our grasp with seven home games and we can't find a way to win one of them. It's a bad feeling. The fans deserve better, ownership deserves better, the front office deserves better, [manager Willie Randolph] and the coaching staff deserve better.

"This is on the players. It's easy to point a finger at somebody. There are twenty-five of us in the clubhouse. We have to look at each other, and that's where the blame is.

"With that being said, there are two big games left. If we go out and win the next two, it puts a lot of pressure on Philadelphia. We know what it's like to be chased. Now all of a sudden, the pressure turns to them."[3]

The Mets seemed inspired by Wright's words. They clobbered Florida, 13–0, the next day. But those same Marlins scored seven runs in the first inning against the Mets on the final day of the season and went on to win the game. The Mets, who had appeared to be a shoo-in to make the playoffs two weeks earlier, were done.

Though Wright stated emphatically that all twenty-five players were to blame, he certainly did his part to keep the Mets alive. While the Mets were collapsing, he embarked on a seventeen-game hitting streak to end the year. During that stretch, he batted a sizzling .397 with 7 doubles, 2 home runs, and 11 RBIs.

The torrid finish capped off a brilliant season in which Wright placed seventh in the National League with a career-best .325 batting average. He also ranked fifth with 113 runs scored, fourth with 196 hits, seventh with 34 stolen bases, and seventh with 94 walks. He led the league with a .360 batting average after the all-star break.

COLLECTING MORE TROPHIES

Equally impressive was that the young man whose defense was considered a weakness earned the Gold Glove award in 2007, signifying his brilliant play at third base. Those who slug home runs receive far more attention than those who are steady in the field. But Wright worked to elevate his overall game. And that meant fielding as well as hitting.

Wright, however, reacted to the news with his typical modesty. "It's not something where I ever at the end of the year expect to win a Gold Glove—or any other individual achievement for that matter," Wright said. "I still think I have a ways to go defensively before I become the defender I want to be.

THE DOUBLES KING

David Wright was so close, but yet so far.

He almost set the Mets' all-time record for doubles in one season. Wright smacked between 40–42 doubles in each of his first four years in the major leagues. The problem is that the team record was forty-four.

Speedy Bernard Gilkey established that mark in 1996.

Wright celebrates his first Gold Glove award with teammates Carlos Beltran and Johan Santana.

"But it's something where I'm honored. It's voted on by your peers and coaches. I'm humbled and was not expecting it. It's going to look good in my trophy case in my apartment. I'm putting in a lot of hours defensively and I still don't think I'm quite there yet."[4]

Wright finished fourth in the National League Most Valuable Player voting and might have won it had his team held on to a playoff spot. But the Mets instead suffered through arguably the greatest collapse in baseball history. And when the final pitch of the year had been thrown, a dejected Wright was not looking forward to going home.

"It's going to be a long off-season," he said. "I know I don't want to experience it again."[5]

Little did he know that 2008 was going to bring more of the same.

10

OH NO! NOT AGAIN!

As much as he would have liked to forget the way the 2007 season ended, David Wright could not.

He preferred to remember "The Great Collapse" in all its misery. It would motivate him to perform better in 2008. And he hoped all his teammates felt the same.

So when the Mets lost two consecutive games to Milwaukee in mid-April, Wright spoke out. He wanted to nip any early-season problems in the bud. And he wanted everyone to know that the current problems were unrelated to the September disaster of the year before.

"Last year has nothing to do with not being able to make pitches," he said. "Last year has nothing to do with not being able to hit with guys in scoring position. It has nothing to do with that. It has to do with our lack of execution. We're not putting away teams when we have the opportunity. We're allowing them to slowly get back into games. That's coming up to bite us."[1]

BACKING UP HIS WORDS

Wright backed up his words with deeds. The following day, he slugged a home run, 2 doubles, and drove in 5 runs to lead the Mets to a 6–0 victory over Washington. Three days later, he slammed 4 hits, including 2 more doubles, in a 6–4 win over Philadelphia. Wright collected 4 singles and 4 doubles in a three-game series against the team that overcame them for the division title in 2007.

THE SUBWAY SERIES

Since 1997, the Major League Baseball regular season schedule has featured a number of interleague games, pitting teams from the American League against teams from the National League.

That gave Mets fans an opportunity to watch their team play the New York Yankees.

Wright rose to the occasion in that heated rivalry in 2008. In a two-game series against the Yankees in mid-May, he contributed 5 hits, including 2 doubles and a home run, and scored 4 runs. In a four-game series against the Yankees in late June, he added 7 hits, one home run and 4 RBIs.

The Mets won five in a row. It appeared they were heating up with the weather, but appearances can be deceiving. For more than a two-month stretch beginning on May 1, they never won more than three consecutive games. After a five-game losing streak that began with a doubleheader loss to Atlanta and ended with a defeat at Colorado on May 23, Wright spoke out again.

He felt that some of his teammates were beginning to accept losing. And accepting losing had always been unacceptable to David Wright. He was frustrated enough to call old friend Paul Lo Duca, who was now with the Washington Nationals, and vent.

"I hope—and this is what I told Paulie—I hope that guys take it personally when we lose," Wright explained. "That's not saying we don't. But I want to get to the point where when we lose it genuinely upsets guys.

"For me, when we lose and I don't play well, it beats me up inside. I play it over and over and over inside my head. For me, that's normal. It's easy for me to do that because I don't have a family. I don't have kids to take my mind away from that. It's twenty-four hours a day for me thinking about what I can do to help this team win."[2]

Wright was performing consistently. After a two-week slump in late April and early May that lowered his batting average to an uncharacteristic .262, he

Wright blasts a two-run homer against the Florida Marlins.

contributed at least one hit in twenty-three of the next twenty-five games to raise that mark to .291. The Mets had become quite dependent on him. In the seven games in which Wright hit a home run during that period, the Mets won six of them.

He could not homer every game. And the Mets were only winning half their games, which was fine for some teams, but not for one with title aspirations.

FAN'S CHOICE

The American League and National League All-Star starting position players are selected by a vote of the fans. The players pick most of the reserve position players while the manager chooses the others, as well as the pitchers.

Wright was voted onto the National League team as a starter in both 2006 and 2007, but was passed over by the fans' vote in 2008. National League manager Clint Hurdle then placed him on the team.

The manager of the All-Star team is the manager of the team from that league that played in the World Series the year before. Hurdle managed the Colorado Rockies into the World Series in 2007.

It is impossible to change your entire team in baseball, so the manager often loses his job when things are not going well. And that's what happened to Mets manager Willie Randolph in mid-June. He was fired and replaced by Jerry Manuel.

The move shocked nobody. But Wright felt badly that Randolph was let go because the players did not perform up to their capabilities.

"I just feel sorry for the guy," Wright said. "We weren't able to play good baseball for him. That's the key."[3]

MOVING FORWARD

They were able to play good baseball for Manuel. They embarked on a ten-game winning streak on July 5 to forge a tie for first place with Philadelphia.

About a month later, Wright heated up at the plate and remained torrid the rest of the season. He slammed 3 hits, including a home run, in a 5–3 win over San Diego on August 7 that kicked off his hot streak and that of the team. The Mets won nineteen of their next twenty-six games as Wright batted .327 with 7 home runs and 19 RBIs.

When the Mets' tear ended on September 3, they were in first place, three games ahead of the Phillies. Once again, it seemed like they were on their way to a division championship, but Wright cautioned that he and his teammates could not afford to tail off again down the stretch.

"I still think we have a long way to go as far as consistency," he said in late August. "But we've become more consistent, and that's why we're the team we are right now and why we are where we are. There's this feeling now on our team that if one guy struggles, another is going to pick him up, and that's the feeling we want to carry all the way through.

"We learned a valuable lesson last year. A lot of them. But the most important is that we have to take care of our own business on a daily basis. We're not going to rely on other teams to ever do our job.

A FALLEN HERO

The most debated baseball issue in early 2008 revolved around Roger Clemens, arguably the greatest pitcher of all time.

Clemens was accused of taking a class of drugs called steroids to help him perform better over the last ten years of his career. He was also accused of lying about it.

Wright, who considered himself a big fan of Clemens growing up and even got his autograph as a child, said he would be disappointed if the accusations turned out to be true.

"Being a player I want to believe Roger," he said. "But as much as I respect him . . . if there's some sort of evidence (that he used steroids), I think he should be punished."

"We don't want to need anybody's help this season. We want to make it on our own."[4]

Wright did his job—and then some. He slammed 10 hits and 4 home runs while driving in 8 runs during one four-game stretch in mid-September. He hit safely in ten consecutive games late that month, smacking 2 hits in seven of those games. He raised his batting average over .300 for the fourth straight year.

But when the Mets were defeated by Florida on September 28, they had been eliminated from the

Manager Jerry Manuel (front), Jose Reyes, and Wright leave after the final game of 2008.

Mets
5
Mets
53

playoffs on the final day of the regular season for the second year in a row. They could have beaten out Milwaukee for the final playoff spot in the National League, but it was not to be.

LOOKING FORWARD

The mood in the clubhouse after that defeat was understandably morose. Players spoke about another opportunity that had escaped them. They knew they were a playoff-caliber team, but championships are won on the field and the Mets simply did not perform well enough to earn a chance at one.

> "We failed as a team. There's no pointing fingers. There's no excuses."
>
> —David Wright

"We failed," Wright stated simply. "We failed as a team. There's no pointing fingers.

ROBERTO CLEMENTE AWARD

After the 2008 season, the Mets placed Wright into nomination for the annual Roberto Clemente Award.

The honor is presented annually to the player in baseball who most understands the value of giving to those less fortunate.

Clemente, who was one of the greatest outfielders in the history of baseball, played for the Pittsburgh Pirates in the 1960s and early 1970s. He was killed in a plane crash on New Year's Eve in 1972 while bringing food and supplies to earthquake victims in his native Nicaragua.

Wright hit a career-high 33 home runs and had 124 RBIs in 2008.

There's no excuses. We as a unit did not get the job done."[5]

Wright never excluded himself from criticism, but many believed he enjoyed his finest season. He finished the 2008 season ranked tenth in the

National League in batting average at .302, ninth in home runs with 33, second in RBIs with 124, seventh in doubles with 42, and fifth in walks with 94. He also cut down significantly on his errors, committing just 16 all season to win another Gold Glove award.

As he watched the Phillies not only beat out his Mets by one game for the division title, but also go on to win the World Series, he could not help but feel a twinge of jealousy. But ever the optimist, Wright saw a silver lining.

"To me, the World Series seems more attainable," he said in early November. "Knowing that a team in your division that you played eighteen or

MEDIA FRENZY

Wright knew he could not expect much privacy from the media when he arrived in New York. After all, there are more newspapers, radio stations, and TV stations in America's largest city than anywhere else.

So he was likely to be interviewed about baseball anywhere.

In fact, as he enjoyed the festivities in mid-November at his fourth annual "Do the Wright Thing Gala," several reporters asked him about what the Mets were doing during the off-season, including his opinion on the possibilities of acquiring particular free agents.

Free agents are players who have played out their contracts with one team and are free to sign with any other team in the major leagues.

nineteen times that you've had pretty good success against went on to win the World Series, I think it gives us an attainable, reachable goal next year."[6]

Wright knows all about goals, both on and off the field. He set a goal to continue his charitable pursuits and was not slowing down a bit. He hosted the fourth annual "Do the Wright Thing Gala" in mid-November 2008, which featured singer David Cook, the reigning winner of the immensely popular TV show *American Idol*. The event raised thousands of dollars for various causes, including the multiple sclerosis centers in the area.

Time and privacy are precious to a professional athlete. Wright could have used his to retreat from the public whenever possible. He could have used his wealth and fame for personal gain. But he chose to use them to cure the sick, feed the hungry, and provide hope for the hopeless.

David Wright has simply followed his heart.

CAREER STATISTICS

Year	Team	Lg	Org.	G	AB	R	H
2001	Kingsport	App	NYM	36	120	27	36
2002	Columbia	SAL	NYM	135	496	85	132
2003	St. Lucie	FSL	NYM	133	466	69	126
2004	Binghamton	East	NYM	60	223	44	81
2004	Norfolk	IL	NYM	31	114	18	34
2004	NY Mets	NL	NYM	69	263	41	77
2005	NY Mets	NL	NYM	160	575	99	176
2006	NY Mets	NL	NYM	154	582	96	181
2007	NY Mets	NL	NYM	160	604	113	196
2008	NY Mets	NL	NYM	160	626	115	189

	G	AB	R	H
Major League Totals - 5 Season(s)	703	2650	464	819
Minor League Totals - 4 Season(s)	395	1419	243	409

KEY:

G – Games
AB – At Bats
R – Runs Scored
H – Hits
2B – Doubles
3B – Triples
HR – Home Runs
RBI – Runs Batted In
BB – Bases on Balls (walks)
SO – Strikeouts
SB – Stolen Bases
CS – Caught Stealing
AVG – Batting Average

2B	3B	HR	RBI	SB	CS	BB	SO	AVG
7	0	4	17	9	1	16	30	.300
30	2	11	93	21	5	76	114	.266
39	2	15	75	19	5	72	98	.270
27	0	10	40	20	6	39	41	.363
8	0	8	17	2	4	16	19	.298
17	1	14	40	6	0	14	40	.293
42	1	27	102	17	7	72	113	.306
40	5	26	116	20	5	66	113	.311
42	1	30	107	34	5	94	115	.325
42	2	33	124	15	5	94	118	.302

2B	3B	HR	RBI	SB	CS	BB	SO	AVG
183	10	130	489	92	22	340	499	.309
111	4	48	242	71	21	219	302	.288

CAREER ACHIEVEMENTS

- Named to Virginia All-State Baseball team, 2000
- Gatorade Virginia High School Player of the Year, 2001
- Virginia All-State Player of the Year, 2001
- Most Valuable Player of Columbia team in South Atlantic League, 2002
- Florida State League All-Star third baseman, 2003
- Reached major leagues with Mets at age 21, July 2004
- Baseball America Second Team Major League All-Star third baseman, 2005
- Ranked 19th among NL Most Valuable Player candidates, 2005

- Mets Player of the Year, 2005
- Ranked ninth among NL Most Valuable Player candidates, 2006
- Starting NL third baseman in All-Star Game, 2006
- Mets Player of the Year, 2007
- NL Silver Slugger Award winner, 2007
- Gold Glove winner, 2007
- National League All-Star, 2007
- National League All-Star, 2008
- Gold Glove winner, 2008

FOR MORE INFORMATION

FURTHER READING

Ross, Allen. *Mets Pride: For the Love of Mookie, Mike and David Wright*. Nashville, Tenn: Cumberland House Publishing, 2007.

Springer, John. *Mets by the Number: A Complete Team History of the Amazin' Mets by Uniform Number*. New York: Skyhorse Publishing, 2008.

WEB LINKS

David Wright Foundation
www.davidwrightfoundation.com

David Wright's MLB player page
mlb.mlb.com/team/player.jsp?player_id=431151

David Wright's page on Baseball-Reference.com
www.baseball-reference.com/w/wrighda03.shtml

CHAPTER NOTES

CHAPTER 1: DETOUR ON ROAD TO STARDOM

1. Personal interview with Hickory High School baseball coach Steve Gedro, September 29, 2008.

2. Vicki L. Friedman, "Senior Eyes Big Leagues, By Way of George Tech," *Virginian-Pilot*, November 24, 2000.

3. Ibid.

4. Ibid.

5. Personal interview with Hickory High School baseball coach Steve Gedro, September 29, 2008.

6. Ibid.

CHAPTER 2: DAVID, THE YOUNG GOLIATH

1. Adam Rubin, "Growing Up Wright," *Sports Illustrated Kids*, 18.7, July 2006, p. T4.

2. Ibid.

3. Frank Lidz, "Prince of the City," *Sports Illustrated*, 104.22, May 29, 2006, p. 44.

4. Ibid.

5. Paul White, "Mets Have the Right Stuff with Wright at Third," *Baseball Digest*, 65.5, July 2006, p. 20.

6. Ibid.

CHAPTER NOTES

CHAPTER 3: GEARING TOWARD GREATNESS

1. Ron Aiken, "The Waiting Game is Over," *The State*, April 4, 2002, p. C1.

2. Ibid.

3. Ibid.

4. Personal interview with Scott Lauber, October 9, 2008.

5. Ibid.

CHAPTER 4: OLD HOME AND NEW HOME

1. Rich Radford, "Wright Move for Tides: Ex-star at Hickory Promoted to Norfolk," *Virginian-Pilot*, June 14, 2004, Sports p. 1.

2. Rich Radford, "He's Wright from the Start," *Virginian-Pilot*, June 15, 2004, Sports p. 1.

3. Rich Radford, "Tides' Wright Is Called up by Mets," *Virginian-Pilot*, July 21, 2004, Sports p. 1.

4. Lee Jenkins, "Rolen Tries to Help Wright Prepare for the Bad Hops," *New York Times*, August 7, 2004, p. D3.

5. Paul White, "Wright: No Hits, but No Complaints," *Virginian-Pilot*, July 22, 2004, p. C1.

CHAPTER 5: EMBRACED IN THE BIG APPLE

1. Lee Jenkins, "Wright's Debut: No Hits, No Gripes," *New York Times*, July 22, 2004, p. D1.

2. Ira Berkow, "Mets' Third Baseman Is Learning to Relax," *New York Times*, August 17, 2004, p. D9.

3. Joe Lapointe, "Wright Brings 'A' Game Even for the Pregame," *New York Times*, July 15, 2005, p. D2.

CHAPTER 6: MORE THAN A BASEBALL STAR

1. Lee Jenkins, "Wright Show Continues, with His Bat as the Star," *New York Times*, August 11, 2005, p. D1.

2. David Amsden, "Mr. Clean: He's Young! Rich! Handsome! Able to Throw Out a Runner at First while Flashing a Killer Smile! David Wright Is the Perfect New York Sports Star – Almost Too Perfect," New York 40.12, April 9, 2007, p. 26(6).

3. Frank Lidz, "Prince of the City," *Sports Illustrated*, 104.22, May 29, 2006, p. 44.

CHAPTER NOTES

CHAPTER 7: DOING THE "WRIGHT" THING

1. Bryan Hoch, "Wright Provides Solid Foundation; Mets Star Steps up in Fight against Multiple Sclerosis," April 1, 2006, news page, <http://www.mlb.com/players/david_wright/foundation/news/index.jsp> (November 4, 2008).

2. Ibid.

3. Bill Harner, "Wright Can Do No Wrong," July 17, 2008, http://www.mlb.com/players/david_wright/news/article.jsp?ymd=20080806&content_id=3262898&vkey=Default&fext=.jsp&c_id=mlb> (November 4, 2008).

4. David Wright Foundation, "Wright, Mets Launch 5 Star*Kids: Star Third Baseman, Club Charity Bringing Youths to Shea," May 16, 2007, news page, <http://www.mlb.com/players/david_wright/foundation/news/index.jsp> (November 4, 2008).

5. Bill Harner, "Wright Can Do No Wrong," July 17, 2008, http://www.mlb.com/players/david_wright/news/article.jsp?ymd=20080806&content_id=3262898&vkey=Default&fext=.jsp&c_id=mlb> (November 4, 2008).

CHAPTER 8: ACHIEVING A DREAM FOR TEAM

1. Frank Lidz, “Prince of the City,” *Sports Illustrated*, 104.22, May 29, 2006, p. 44.

2. Jarret McNeill, “David Wright: He's Young, He's Handsome, He Receives Marriage Proposals in the Mail, and He Plays Infield for New York's Best Team. Derek Jeter Should Be So Lucky,” Interview 36.8, September 2006, p. 138.

3. Associated Press, “Mets Sign Wright to Six-Year $55M Extension,” August 8, 2006. <http://sports.espn.go.com/mlb/news/story?id=2541623> (November 10, 2008)

4. Associated Press, “Green Helps Mets Break Out Broom on Dodgers in NLDS,” October 7, 2006, <http://sports.espn.go.com/mlb/recap?gameId=261007119> (November 10, 2008).

CHAPTER 9: GREAT SEASON, SAD ENDING

1. Mike Zimmerman, “Your Breakout Season,” *Men's Health* 22.3, April 2007, p. 129-137.

2. David Amsden, “Mr. Clean: He's Young! Rich! Handsome! Able to Throw Out a Runner at First while Flashing a Killer Smile! David Wright Is the Perfect New York Sports Star – Almost Too Perfect,” New York 40.12, April 9, 2007, p. 26(6).

3. Jorge Arangure, Jr., “Wright's Challenging Words Might Be Too Late,” Sept. 28, 2007, <http://sports.espn.go.com/mlb/news/story?id=3041710> (November 11, 2008).

CHAPTER NOTES

4. Adam Rubin, "A-Rod Who? David Wright Wins Gold Glove," New York Daily News online, November 7, 2007, <http://www.nydailynews.com/sports/baseball/mets/2007/11/07/2007_11_arod_who_david_wright_wins_gold_glove.html> (November 11, 2008).

5. Associated Press, "Glavine Allows Seven Runs in First as Mets End on Sour Note," September 30, 2007, <http://sports.espn.go.com/mlb/recap?gameId=270930121> (November 11, 2008).

CHAPTER 10: OH NO! NOT AGAIN!

1. Adam Rubin, "Age and Memories Add to Mets' Malaise," New York Daily News online, April 14, 2008, <http://www.nydailynews.com/sports/baseball/mets/2008/04/14/2008-04-14_age_and_memories_add_to_mets_malaise.html> (November 12, 2008).

2, Ben Shpigel, "Wright Wants Mets to Take Losses Personally," New York Times online, May 24, 2008, <http://nytimes.com/2008/05/24/sports/baseball/24shea.html > (October 28, 2008).

3. New York Daily News staff, "Mets Players React to Randolph's Firing." New York Daily News online, June 18, 2008, <http://www.nydailynews.com/sports/baseball/mets/2008/06/17/2008-06-17_mets_players_react_to_randolphs_firing-1.html> (November 12, 2008).

4. Mike Lupica, "Time Is Now for David Wright and Mets," New York Daily News online, August 23, 2008, <http://www.nydailynews.com/sports/baseball/mets/2008/08/23/2008-08-23_time_is_now_for_david_wright_and_mets.html> (November 12, 2008).

5. Associated Press, "Another Collapse Befalls Mets as Bullpen Allows Key Homers," September 28, 2008, <http://sports.espn.go.com/mlb/recap?gameId=290928121> (November 12, 2008).

6. Mark Lelinwalla, "Phillies Give David Wright, Mets a New World View," New York Daily News online, November 1, 2008, <http://www.nydailynews.com/sports/baseball/mets/2008/11/01/2008-11-01_phillies_give_david_wright_mets_a_new_wo.html> (November 12, 2008).

GLOSSARY

American League—One of the two major leagues, consisting of fourteen teams and three divisions.

at-bat—Any time at the plate for a batter that results in a base hit, error or out.

batting average—A measure of a hitter's achievement calculated by his number of at-bats divided by his number of hits. A .300 batting average is considered very good.

double—A hit in which the runner reaches second base safely.

home run—A hit that travels over the fence and allows the runner to trot around the bases and touch home plate for a run.

major leagues—The American League and National League combined.

manager—The person most responsible for the team on the field, including the daily lineup and strategic moves made during games.

minor leagues—A group of teams in various leagues owned by major-league organizations that provides a feeder system to the major-league teams.

National League—One of the two major leagues, consisting of sixteen teams and three divisions.

RBI—The abbreviation for "run batted in," which is achieved when a batter gets a hit or a fly ball that allows a runner to score.

regular season—The 162-game schedule played by major-league teams.

scholarship—The financial offer to a high school athlete by a university, including tuition, for the purpose of attracting that athlete to that school.

scout—A representative from a college or professional sports team who tries to find athletes to convince them to sign contracts to play for their school or professional organization.

shortstop—The defender who plays on the left side of the infield between the second baseman and third baseman.

slugger—A slang word for an accomplished batter who hits a lot of home runs and doubles.

GLOSSARY

spring training—A six-week period in February and March in which baseball players and teams prepare for the regular season.

stolen base—The act of moving up a base by running and reaching it before being tagged out by an infielder who has received a throw from the catcher. The most common stolen base is second.

third baseman—The defender who plays on the far left of the infield, generally close to the third-base bag.

walk-off home run—A home run that ends a game.

World Series—The annual best-of-seven series in late October pitting the American League champions against the National League champions to decide the Major League Baseball title.

INDEX

INDEX

INDEX